CATS JUST KNOW

Written by M.H. Clark | Illustrated by Emily Taylor

Cats know that sometimes doing nothing
is the most important thing.

Cats know that the world is full of wonders,
just here for the noticing.

Cats know you should savor every day
and its little luxuries.

Cats know you should keep your wildness,
your strangeness, and your mystery.

Cats know you should take impeccable care of yourself.

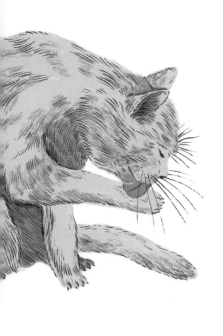

*Because then, you can take
impeccable care of everyone else.*

*Cats know life's perfect moments
are the ones we spend together.*

Cats know we are here for each other.
And that love changes us for the better.

Cats know you have to be true to yourself,

and do the things your heart calls you to do.

*Cats know that what seems impossible
might just need a little follow-through.*

Cats know that adventure is waiting to be found—
in every single day, if you just look around.

Cats know that sometimes in life, you need to take a risk.
(Because usually, it's worth it.)

Cats know you should make up your own mind,
and go your own way.
(Cats know you get to shape each minute,
each hour, and each day.)

Cats know that we don't have to do everything perfectly...

And that we're more resilient
than we might have believed.

Cats know that the little things are the magic life is made of.

And that the little gestures are the biggest show of love.

Cats know that almost everything
can be fixed with a nudge and a purr.
(Cats even suspect this is why they are here.)

Cats know how wonderful it is to simply coexist.
Because cats know that presence is the best gift there is.

Cats just know what matters most.
And then, they teach us too.

Cats change us for the better,
with everything they do.

COMPENDIUM.
live inspired

Written by: M.H. Clark
Illustrated by: Emily Taylor
Edited by: Bailey Vega
Art Directed by: Chelsea Bianchini

ISBN: 978-1-957891-27-9

1st printing. Printed in China with soy inks on FSC®-Mix certified paper.

*Create
meaningful
moments
with gifts
that inspire.*

CONNECT WITH US
live-inspired.com | sayhello@compendiuminc.com

    @compendiumliveinspired
#compendiumliveinspired